? ( ) " " . ; ! , ? ( ) " " , .

Punctuation summary

This shows you the different punctuation marks, each with its name and an example in which it is used. You will find out all about them as you work through this book. Check that you can recognize them all, then do the puzzle below.

.	full stop	They have seen some shirts they want.	
,	comma	I like chicken, sausages and chocolate.	
:	colon	Here's what you must bring: a swimsuit, a towel and a sandwich.	
;	semicolon	The view is fine; the broken window is the problem.	
?	question mark	Who is that?	
!	exclamation mark	That video is so stupid!	
'	apostrophe	Sarah's hat	
" "	quotation marks	He said, "Please wait for us by the fountain."	
( )	brackets	Win a luxury holiday for two (details next week).	
-	hyphen	I am a little short-sighted.	
–	dash	It is not a problem – just inconvenient.	
A B C	capital letters	At first, we found King Pong scary.	

Testing correspondence

How many of each of the following are there in this letter: full stops, commas, colons, semicolons, exclamation marks, hyphens, quotation marks, question marks and apostrophes?

The Select Residential College
Blimpton-on-Sea
3 September 2000

Dear Mr and Mrs Fishplaite,

It is my sad duty to write to you regarding your daughter, Sonia, whom we must ask you to withdraw from S.R.C.

Sonia's attitude and manners have dramatically deteriorated: the poor quality of her work does nothing to compensate for this.

The events which prompted the decision are as follows: she locked her French teacher, Mademoiselle Ragou, in a cupboard and called her "an unenlightened stick-insect". She later called me "a Komodo dragon" in front of all the girls and my staff at morning assembly!

We will of course help you in any way possible, and Sonia can remain here until the end of term. Would you like us to obtain a place for her at Highwall College, an establishment with the strong, disciplinarian approach which your daughter needs?

I look forward to hearing from you in the very near future.

Yours sincerely,

K.D. Brittledge

Katrina Diana Brittledge
Headmistress

The full stop is the dot which you normally find at the end of a sentence. But it has several other uses too.

I just heard a cuckoo.

full stop

Ending a sentence

A sentence is a group of words that can stand on its own and make sense. It starts with a capital letter and must have a full stop at the end, unless you are using a question mark or an exclamation mark (see below).

A full stop at the end of a sentence stands for a clear pause. It shows where, if you were speaking, your voice would drop and you would stop for a moment.

Here are the only two cases in which you do not use a full stop to end a sentence:

1 If a sentence is a question, it must end with a question mark, not a full stop. For example: *Which gate number do I go to?* This is explained on page 12.

2 If a sentence is about a strong feeling, you can end it with an exclamation mark: I hate that! (See page 14.)

Sentence spotting

In order to know where to put full stops, you have to be able to spot a sentence.

To qualify as a sentence, a group of words must make sense when it stands on its own. A typical sentence has a subject (a person or thing doing the action) and a verb (an action word): *The postman opened the parcel.*

Sentences can be very short, though, and their meaning then depends on other sentences around them. Look at this example: *What did you say? Nothing.* Here, "nothing" is a sentence. If you know what was said before, it makes sense, and so it ends with a full stop.

Sentences can be linked with words like *and, but, so* or *because* to become one longer sentence, with a single full stop at the end. For example: *The postman opened the parcel and the counterfeit money fell out.*

Shortening words

You can put a full stop at the end of an abbreviation (a short form of a word), where it stands for the letters that you have not written out. For example:

	stands for
m.p.h.	miles per hour
U.N.	United Nations
J. Thomas	The initial, or first letter, J stands for the person's first name, John.

If an abbreviation is at the end of a sentence, use only one full stop: *She works for the U.N.*

The full stop after an abbreviation is optional. For example, both U.N. and UN are correct*. Use one whenever it helps to make your writing clear: for example, Mon. morning is clearer than Mon morning.

With words such as Mister that are shortened to their first and last letters, you do not use a full stop: for example, *Mr Thomas.*

── **Pen problems** ──

This message has six full stops, but it also has black ink splodges that look like full stops. Copy it out, keeping only the six correct full stops.

I'll be home. late from school today, Mum. After volleyball practice, Miss. Mussly wants to discuss plans for our sports day. See you at about 6. p.m.. (Please. feed Misty as soon as you get in. Because of the kittens, I don't think. she should have to wait until 6.)

*For abbreviations which people read out as if they were words, such as UNESCO (which is said you-ness-coe), you normally do not use full stops.

Improve your Punctuation

Nicole Irving

Designed by Isaac Quaye
Illustrated by Colin Mier

Educational consultants:
Valerie Munro and Phillipa Ferst

CONTENTS

When you are writing, do you ever wonder if you need a comma (,) or an apostrophe ('), and where to put them? If so, you can find out more in this book. These marks are part of punctuation. If you do all the puzzles in this book, good punctuation will become second nature. On the way, clear rules and tips will help you learn how to use each mark.

What is punctuation for?

Punctuation is a set of marks that you use in writing to divide up groups of words and make them easier to read.

When speaking, you vary the speed and loudness of words. In writing, punctuation shows these variations. It helps make the meaning clear because it shows how you would say the words, as well as where sentences begin, slow down and end.

See how the meaning changes depending on the punctuation you use:

Sam and Lucy, don't eat all that junk food!

Sam and Lucy don't eat all that junk food.

Without punctuation, even words that can only have one meaning are hard to read. Compare these letters, for instance:

dear mrs peters
my dog lucky has disappeared i think i heard him barking inside your garage so i think he has got stuck in there i would really appreciate your help in finding my dog please ring me or my dad when you get home
tina

Dear Mrs Peters,
My dog Lucky has disappeared. I think I heard him barking inside your garage, so I think he has got stuck in there.
I would really appreciate your help in finding my dog. Please ring me or my Dad when you get home.
Tina

Punctuation is a vital writing skill. You need this skill to ensure that your writing is clear. It is also essential if you want to write more than very basic English.

Using this book

This book looks at each punctuation mark in turn. Read through the guidelines, then test your punctuation skills by trying the puzzles which follow.

The book is not designed for writing in, so have some paper and a pen ready for your answers. You can check these at the back of the book.

Don't worry if you make mistakes. Work through the puzzles, then go back to anything you found hard.

You will come across a few grammatical terms, such as *subject, verb* etc. You can use the index on page 32 to find out where each term is explained.

How much punctuation?

SAM!!!!

In cartoon strips, you sometimes see lots of punctuation. This is because there is not enough room to explain the atmosphere and the characters' feelings. Extra punctuation is used instead.

Avoid using this much. Use enough for your meaning to be clear and no more. To show that someone said something in a particular way, describe how they said it, instead of relying on punctuation. For example: *"Sam!" he called angrily.*

The book explains the rules you should follow. In formal writing, such as essays and letters to people you don't know well, keep close to the rules. In other situations, you can be more flexible. If you are unsure, write short sentences. They are much easier to punctuate than long ones.

im.   The train is late.   I like sausages.   *That is mine.*

Costly dots

Freddy is trying to write a message. He must add three full stops. Where should he put these to make his message as clear as possible?

> SORRY I LET YOU DOWN IN INVERNESS I'LL EXPLAIN WHEN I SEE YOU MY MONEY BELT WAS STILL IN YOUR BACKPACK WHEN YOU LEFT IN A HUFF PLEASE MEET ME FORT WILLIAM STATION ON SAT 8PM RIGHT OF LEFT-LUGGAGE LOCKERS.

Pointless

Five of these pieces of writing are sentences which should end with a full stop. Decide which they are, and then write them out, ending each one with a full stop**.

1   **Further up the coast, the explorer**
2   **In Japan, cats have no tails**
3   **They were**
4   **All of a sudden, it vanished**
5   **They suffered dreadfully from cold, hunger**
6   **He cannot go into**
7   **It all seemed highly**
8   **She grabbed the mobile phone, lurched forward and**
9   **Sam looked blank**
10 **In front of her**

Drifter's diary

This diary extract is written with no full stops at all. Write it out, adding as many full stops as possible and making sure that each sentence starts with a capital letter.

Monday

up at 11 am I didn't wash my sisters had left the bathroom in such a state that I didn't feel like it I went over to Jo Drone's Café for a hotdog because Dad was retiling the kitchen floor I just love that hot yellow mustard Teeny Tina came by for me later and we spent the whole afternoon at the DJ Club on my way home I bumped into my old classmate Sally Straite in Suburb Lane when I told her about how bored I felt, she told me to pull myself together and perhaps get a summer job she suggested I start by keeping a diary Sally thinks that the problems I have to iron out will soon become clear all I have to do is keep a diary for a few days and then read it through she reckons the problems will soon leap off the page at me

Sally's tel number is 666 3333 she said I can ring her whenever I need some moral support I'm going to clean up the bathroom now then I'm going to have a bath and go to bed it's 10 pm

Dotty dramas

The police are investigating a train robbery. They have received some information from an anonymous witness, but it is difficult to make sense of, as there is not much punctuation. Split it up into sentences, using full stops and capital letters.

I read the article in yesterday's Echo about the great pearl robbery I was on that train and am writing to let you know what I know there were hardly any passengers on the train in my carriage there was only one man I noticed him because he had six briefcases and looked very nervous I soon dozed off all of a sudden I woke up to the sound of terrible shouts a woman with a black mask over her face rushed towards me and threw a pile of prawn and mayonnaise sandwiches in my face and all over my clothes then she climbed out of the window onto the platform the woman disappeared into the night while I started trying to wipe off the prawns and

mayonnaise at this point I discovered there were lots of blue pearls mixed in with the food I scraped as much as I could into a plastic bag and got off the train nobody noticed me go in all the commotion now that I have read about what happened to the man with the briefcases I want to hand in the pearls you can phone me on 867 2382

**The hints on page 4 on how to spot a sentence will help you.

The comma stands for a short pause that separates a word or group of words from another in a sentence. You normally use it where you would pause very slightly if you were speaking. Commas are often essential to make the meaning clear.

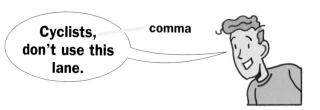

Cyclists, don't use this lane.

comma

Cyclists don't use this lane has another meaning from the sentence above.

Commas in lists

When you list words in a sentence, use commas to separate them. Normally, if the last two parts of the list are joined with *and*, you don't put a comma in front of *and*. For example: *These are made from eggs, flour, water, cheese and herbs.*

Sometimes, though, you need a comma in front of *and*, to make sure the sentence is clear: *Jim ordered tomato soup, cheese, and coffee ice cream.* The comma makes clear that he did not order *cheese and coffee ice cream*!

When you list adjectives (describing words) before a noun (a naming word), commas between the adjectives are not always needed. In *deep, cold pond*, the comma sounds best. In *big blue eyes*, it is unnecessary. Put commas in when it would be natural to pause*.

Long sentences

To know where commas go in long sentences, it helps to know how sentences are made. A typical one has at least one main clause (this has a subject and a verb, makes sense on its own, and could itself be a sentence). It may also have 1) a subordinate clause – this too has a verb, but depends on a main clause for its meaning; 2) a phrase – this adds meaning; it is often short and says where, when or how something happens.

Comma or no comma?

Here are some rules and guidelines on when to use commas in long sentences:

1 Put a comma in front of words like *but, although, so, yet* and *or* when you use them to link main clauses. For example: *It is a tough journey, so plan carefully**.*

Leave out the comma when linking main clauses with *and*: *Our ship docked and the officers came aboard.* Put a comma in, though, if *and* introduces a new idea (*This is good news, and I shall pass it on*), or if it is needed for clarity.

2 Use a comma to separate off a phrase at the start of a sentence: *After this row, they felt better.* After a short phrase, the comma is optional.

If the phrase comes later, you may need commas on either side of it in order to make the meaning clear: *She whistled and luckily her dog followed* (commas are optional). *She whistled and, after a tiff with a passing cat, her dog followed* (commas here are best).

3 Commas may be needed to separate a subordinate clause from a main clause. If the subordinate clause is first, a comma is usual: *While Zoe wrote, Pip washed up.*

4 For a subordinate clause starting with *who, whom* or *which*, a comma must separate it off if it is not essential to the meaning. Leaving out the comma makes the clause a more important part of the sentence, and so may change its meaning. For example:

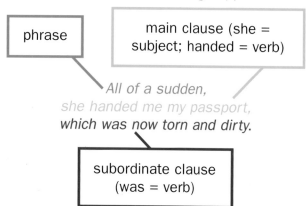

phrase

main clause (she = subject; handed = verb)

All of a sudden, she handed me my passport, which was now torn and dirty.

subordinate clause (was = verb)

He threw away the eggs, which were broken.

He threw away the eggs which were broken.

*The comma can affect the meaning: compare *a pretty small girl* (quite small) with *a pretty, small girl* (pretty and small).
**In informal writing, people often leave out the comma when linking short main clauses: *It is tough so plan carefully.*

the island, **dolls, puppets and robots** *early that day,*

Two by two

For each pair of pictures below, there are two sentences. Match each sentence with the correct picture.

The apples, which were red, had worms in them.

The apples which were red had worms in them.

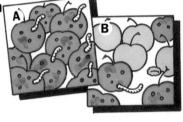
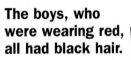

The boys, who were wearing red, all had black hair.

The boys who were wearing red all had black hair.

The ham, which was cold, came with salad.

The ham which was cold came with salad.

A comma or two

Copy out these sentences, adding one comma each to sentences 1 - 4, and two commas each to sentences 5 - 9.

1 **My brother is lazy rude and arrogant.**
2 **Many people will read this story although it is very badly written.**
3 **Stefie has brought flowers ice cream and chocolates.**
4 **Meanwhile Susie was cycling home.**
5 **I took the books which were old torn and shabby but left the good ones for my mother.**
6 **The three bands that were playing were Sound and Emotion Billy and the Cheesemakers and the Blue Moon Band.**
7 **He waved at Lisa who was watching from the window and walked down the street.**
8 **The rugby players who were exhausted limped off the pitch together.**

Lily's list

Lily has written out her shopping list without putting any commas in. Can you add 14 commas?

Chemist's:
new toothbrush aspirin and soap.
Butcher's:
sausages bacon and a leg of lamb.
Supermarket:
milk butter eggs flour sugar pasta tins of sardines and ice cream.
Greengrocer's:
apples pears bananas beans carrots and broccoli.
Baker's:
five bread rolls and two loaves of bread.
Hardware shop:
six short sturdy nails and a small hammer.

Comma commotion

There are too many commas in this cutting from a catalogue. Rewrite the descriptions, taking out 11 commas that should not be there.

These Cosifit ear muffs are warm, comfortable, and suitable for anyone from 6 to 60! The adjustable head strap means that however, big or small your head may be, Cosifit ear muffs, will always fit!

This latest addition to the Supertec, computer, game series is the most exciting, challenging and absorbing, yet! Can you help Hoghero in his desperate battle, for control of the universe? Help him stop nasty Miteymouse, from conquering the world!

Every trendy, teenager needs a Staralarm! When you go to bed, just set the alarm by choosing a time and a voice - the voice of your favourite, pop star. What better way to wake up than to the sound of Kool Malone, Freddy, and the Freezers, or Ritchy Roon?

Dot dot dot

You use three full stops in a row (...) to show that some words are missing, or that a sentence is unfinished:

I must not get these shoes...

Tinker, tailor, soldier... beggarman, thief.

You should not use three full stops after expressions such as *and so on* and *et cetera*. People sometimes do, but a single full stop here is correct.

Numbers

In maths, the full stop is used as the decimal point (as in *1.5* to mean *one and a half*). Always write the decimal point very clearly, as the difference between, for example, 1.5 and 15 is enormous.

In most written English, the comma is used to break up numbers that are over four figures long, for example, 10,000. You start from the right and put a comma in after each set of three numerals. This helps to make it easier to read long numbers. You do not normally do this in maths and science.

Comma tips

Page 6 explains how to use commas*. Sometimes, though, it is hard to decide where to put them. Here are two tips:

1 Make sure each complete sentence ends with a full stop, then try reading aloud, listening out for natural pauses. For each pause, think whether a comma is needed.
2 If you still do not know where to put the commas, perhaps your sentence is too complicated or too long, and needs rewriting.

Look at this example: *Mrs Fern, the head of my old school and the piano teacher who, years ago, gave my brother lessons, left to go to work in a circus.*

In order to say that Mrs Fern, who is a former headmistress and piano teacher, went to work in a circus, you must rewrite the sentence. At present, because too many details are attached to the main information, the sentence could mean that Mrs Fern, the headmistress and the former piano teacher (three

different people) went to work in a circus. A comma before *and the teacher* will not help.

Here is a possible rewrite: *Mrs Fern, who was the head of my old school and was also the piano teacher who, years ago, gave my brother lessons, left to go to work in a circus.*

To do the puzzles on these two pages, you may need to look back at pages 3 and 5.

Mix and match

Here are eight sentences, each cut in two. By looking at the capital letters, full stops and commas, see if you can match up the sixteen pieces to make the eight most suitable sentences.

but I still could not make up my mind.

, then grudgingly guided them down the dark alley.

I thought it over

After the detective's visit

In the late afternoon,

, which is in Canada.

Andy and his parents have moved to Gap,

and quickly decided on a course of action.

The woman looked down her nose at them,

I decided to go to the police station.

He gave me some sound advice,

which is in France.

, I no longer felt in the mood to work.

The man wrinkled up his nose in disdain

Jan and her family have moved to Arcola

but agreed to show them the documents.

*Commas are also used in letter writing (see page 24) and in direct speech, such as *I said, "Come back!"* (see page 20).

Internet link: For a link to a website where you can test yourself on punctuation, spelling and grammar, with some fun online quizzes, go to **www.usborne-quicklinks.com**

dog is a small... The essential That is mine. Milk, flour, eggs...

Stop gap

Copy out these sentences, using five full stops, eleven commas and a set of three dots (...) to complete them.

1 **Live coverage of this fascinating sporting event will begin on Radio Livewire at 6**

2 **There were 18000 people at the concert so our chances of bumping into Gemma Jim and Sam were very slight**

3 **Disheartened the explorers began their return journey setting off**

4 **In early Roman times theatres were built of wood**

5. **At last wet gasping and exhausted they reached the bus shelter**

6 **The sun which we had not seen for two months blinded us**

Printer problems

This printer prints three dots wherever a full stop or a comma is needed, as well as where three full stops are correct. Copy the text out, replacing the three dots with full stops and commas wherever you think would be best.

Tennessee Open Zoo Wild Cats Leaflet

Nearly all wild cats live in rainforests... They hunt and eat meat... They have very good eyesight... and often...
   (Cathy... please research all the general points for the above opening paragraph... When you have done so... write them up on my computer... The file name is WCL...)
   The tiger is the largest cat... It is extremely strong... It hunts for its food... catching large animals if it can... Rather than go hungry... though... it eats small creatures such as frogs... ants... worms... beetles and so on...
   (Cathy... please also research and write the section on leopards... I have gathered the relevant books... folders... cuttings... etc... You will find them all on my desk... to the left of the pile of parrot leaflets...)

Hasty homework

This essay has full stops and capital letters, but no other punctuation. Copy it out, adding commas where needed (the photos may help you).

<u>My summer holiday</u>
For my summer holiday I went to Agadir a beach paradise in Morocco. I stayed in a luxury hotel with three enormous swimming pools a cinema two discos a jogging track and a computer games room.
   The hotel is by a beautiful long white beach and the bedrooms which have balconies overlook the sea. My Mum and Dad had a hard time getting to sleep because of the waves crashing down below. My room which had no balcony and was just around the corner was quiet.
   I did not like the pools as much as the sea although they did have lots of truly awesome water rapids waves and whirlpools. The two swimming pools which have lots of sun-loungers around them are always crowded. Because the third one has lanes in it for serious swimming it is usually empty. On the beach there were huge waves which I loved. One morning after a storm I saw some jellyfish on the beach.
   The food was brilliant. The hotel has chefs from all over the world so we mostly ate Chinese food and Moroccan food which were our favourites.
   Even though we only spent a day there our visit to Marrakesh was the highlight of the whole holiday. It is a really exciting town and the markets and tiny ancient streets are full of weird things like carpets olives and spices all piled up leather bags and sandals.
   Because it was spring and the weather was not too hot I really enjoyed this holiday.

colon

Make sure you pack the following items: map, compass, torch, whistle and waterproof jacket.

semicolon

Rehearsing this piece of music is good fun; performing it in front of people is the problem.

The colon is two dots, one above the other. The semicolon is made of a dot over a comma. Both of them represent a pause in a sentence (a longer pause than shown by a comma and a shorter one than shown by a full stop). They are not followed by a capital letter.

The semicolon

This has two main uses:

1 It can separate two closely linked main clauses* of similar importance. It is used instead of a full stop or a word like *and* or *but*. For example: *He lifted the lid; the lost gems fell out.*

In this example, the semicolon gives a dramatic effect of short, linked pieces. Using a full stop instead, the effect would be jerky: *He lifted the lid. The lost gems fell out.* With *and*, it would be less dramatic:

He lifted the lid and the lost gems fell out.

If using a semicolon seems tricky, just avoid it. A practical tip is to think of using one before words such as *besides*, *consequently*, *therefore*, *even so*, *still*, *otherwise* and *moreover* when these link two main clauses. For example: *Their train was late; even so, they got the connection.*

2 The semicolon is also used to break up the different items in a list.

Normally, you use commas for this (see page 6). But if the items in the list are long and complicated (which often means they need commas themselves), you use semicolons instead. For example: *To make this bag, you will need a large, sturdy needle for sewing tough fabrics; extremely thick thread made of nylon or some sort of synthetic material; coarse, rip-stop grey fabric with the logo printed on it; and finally, a white button of any sort**.*

The colon

The colon does two things:

1 It can introduce a list of items. For example: *To build a model train tunnel, you will need: a shoe box, sandpaper, paints and glue.* You can also write a list with no colon (*...you will need a shoe box, sandpaper...*). By drawing attention to the start of the list, the colon helps make the writing clear.

In two cases, the colon is essential:
a) when the list is laid out as a column.
You will need:
a shoe box
sandpaper
paints
glue.

b) when the list begins *You will need the following*: or *Here is a checklist of things you should do*: or expressions like this. In cases like these, you can tell that you need a colon before the start of the list itself because you cannot read on without a pause.

2 The colon can go between two main clauses to introduce an explanation or a summary of the first clause:
We soon solved the mystery of the missing sausages: the dog had helped himself. (explanation)
As she read the letter, she grinned and hugged everyone: she was over the moon with joy. (summary)

*This is the part of a sentence that contains a subject and a verb, and which makes sense on its own.
**Here a semicolon is used before *and finally*, but a comma would be possible instead.

Internet link: For a link to a website where you can watch a short movie about colons and semicolons, go to **www.usborne-quicklinks.com**

Fishy prizes

Here are the three winning entries in a cookery competition. To make the recipes clear, where in each one should you add two colons, a comma and a semicolon?

First Prize

Quiche Marine – For the pastry, you will need flour, butter or margarine, one egg.

For the filling, have ready the following fresh prawns, shelled; crab meat either fresh or from a tin cream, eggs and seasoning.

Make the pastry in the usual way, roll it out and line a flan dish with it. Mix the ingredients for the filling, pour them onto the pastry and bake for 25 minutes.

Second Prize

Perfect Fish Pie – To make the potato layer, mix together some mashed potatoes, milk and eggs.

For the fish layer, get the following mixture ready: chopped fresh plaice, sole and salmon in equal quantities. Mix these together, adding a dash of salt and a squeeze of lemon juice.

The ingredients for the cheese sauce are equal amounts of milk, cream and yogurt; a tablespoon of flour; finely grated cheddar cheese; two beaten egg yolks. Stir these together in a pan, heating gently until thick. Don't include the cheese this must go in after the sauce has thickened and is off the heat.

To assemble the pie do the following: put half the potato in the bottom of an ovenproof dish; place the fish mixture on top, making sure it is well spread over all the potato; cover with the remaining potato finally, pour the cheese sauce over the top and bake for 30 minutes. Serve with a green salad.

Young Chef of the Month

*A prize for entries from cooks aged **11 or under**.*

Green Fishcakes with Pink Sauce – For the fishcakes, mash together these ingredients poached cod, boiled potatoes and two raw eggs. Add a mixture of finely chopped fresh herbs. Include parsley and chives, and one of the following dill, fennel, sorrel. Also add a knob of butter. Shape this mixture into fishcakes and fry gently in a little butter and corn oil.

For the sauce mince some peeled shrimps and mix with lots of sour cream.

When the fishcakes are ready, heat the sauce and pour it into the plates. Place the fishcakes on top of the sauce. As a main course, serve with boiled new potatoes and broccoli as a starter, serve with crusty bread.

Getting it right

Copy out these ads, adding either a colon or a semicolon to each.

Washomatic for sale. This machine is a genuine bargain: it is only 12 years old; there is not a single visible patch of rust on it last but not least, it does not leak. Phone Johnny on 324 5543.

Attention, old pen collectors! Green Silhouette pen for sale. 1952 model. Features included original case, gold nib, embossed logo. Phone Pipa Pentop. 324 5682.

For sale or hire garage in Bach Alley. Contact Mrs Lucas, 3 Bach Square.

Wanted young person to deliver newspapers in Combe Park area. Must have own bike. Apply to Nat's News.

Gardener sought. The following qualifications are required familiarity with Supermow, sound knowledge of organic vegetable growing and garden pest control. Phone 324 3344.

Hair excesses

Copy out these pieces of writing, taking out the surplus punctuation. Each one has an unnecessary colon or semicolon.

Come to us: for a wide range of hair care: perms, hair straightening, colour change, highlights, beading, hair extensions.

Our perms are perfect in every way: gentle, lasting; and adapted to suit your face shape.

Choose between three wonderful shampoos: frosted yogurt and banana for dry hair; lemon and lime cocktail for greasy hair; finally, for problem hair, mango and chilli revitalizing magic; or Brazil nut balsam.

Always follow up a shampoo with a good conditioner: this guarantees good hair condition. Amongst our dozens of choices, we recommend either: deep action strawberry, marigold petal extract or luxury oatmilk.

Treat yourself to: a head massage, the ideal treatment for tired heads. You get a 15 minute massage given by an expert; generous amounts of the best massage oils; a shampoo and blow dry.

We give you the hair shape you want. Once you have it, you will want to keep it; to help you, we stock 30 varieties of hair spray. Also in stock: hundreds of lacquers, hair gels; and waxes.

The question mark is a sign that goes on the end of a sentence which asks a question. It shows where, in speech, you would raise your voice a little, then pause as for a full stop.

> Can you hear me?

question mark

Direct questions

The kind of question which ends with a question mark is called a direct question. It is a question to which an answer is expected. This is how typical direct questions look:

> They begin with a capital letter.

Are you tired?*

first word is a verb or a question word (see right)

subject comes after the verb

Why are you tired?

> They end with a question mark.

Longer questions may begin with extra words, but the order (verb/subject or question word/verb/subject) is the same. For example: *So then, why are you tired?*

Direct questions can be very short and have no verb or subject. For example: *Why?*

As the question mark is used instead of a full stop, you put a capital letter after it: *Why are you tired? It is only ten o'clock.*

Indirect questions

An indirect question is a type of sentence which looks a little like a direct question but is a normal sentence. It ends with a full stop, not a question mark. Here is an example: *She is asking if you can hear.*

It is a sentence which tells you about a question that was asked. You can think of it as a reported question.

To spot an indirect question, look for expressions like *ask* or *wonder* used with *if, whether* or a question word (see above right). Notice too that the word order is subject/verb (*you can*), not the other way around (*can you*) as for a direct question.

Question words

Here are the most commonly used question words:

> Whose?
> Whom? Where? Why?
> What? Who?
> When? Which?
> How?

Some of these words are not used only in questions. They can double up as other kinds of words. For example: *When I was on the ferry, I felt ill.*

Question tags

Question tags are short and are tagged onto the end of a statement, after a comma: *You play the violin, don't you?* These question tags belong to spoken English, so avoid them in formal writing such as essays. However, if you write one, remember that it turns the sentence into a question, so put a question mark on the end.

——Ask a straight question——

How many of the following are direct questions that need a question mark, and how many are indirect ones that don't?

1   **I asked her if she could bring him to my party**
2   **Can you bring your brother to my party**
3   **Does anyone know where I put my watch**
4   **Is there a sweet shop around here**
5   **Did you ask if there is a sweet shop around here**
6   **When do you think you will be able to help out on the school magazine**
7   **Will you be able to help out on the school magazine**
8   **Who do you feel we could invite along**

*In very informal, spoken English, questions are sometimes made without moving the verb: *You're tired?*
If you write down a question like this, for example in a note, put a question mark on the end.

Internet link: *For a link to a website where you can play a game and see if you know how to use punctuation marks, go to* **www.usborne-quicklinks.com**

 here are they going?　　Is there a problem?　　Can you help?

Awkward questions

Each of the ten questions on this police report have been printed in jumbled order. Can you work out what the questions might be? (They are all direct questions.)

1　live you here Do?

2　night were eleven Where at o'clock last you?

3　with who TV are of friends were What watching the the you names four ?

4　unusual Did your you friends or of anything hear one?

5　you friend a Jack have Do called?

6　night here Was last he?

7　heard around you who the Gang, gang the Have a of of hang Burly thugs neighbourhood?

8　their them you to leader or Jack ever about Hasn't boasted mentioned being?

9　heard unusual if asked when Why lie I you you you had anything did?

10　so it Was Jack you he parents' night who could gave your garage key to hide there the last?

Searching questions

Help Jan enter a songwriting competition. Copy the lyrics she has written, adding full stops or question marks to the ends of the seven lines that need them.

One day, you'll leave, won't you
When I asked you last summer,
　　You said you'd be true,
　　But now, I just wonder

　　Why is it always me
　　That gets left behind
In this state, I can't see
How life can ever be kind

　　Friends are no better
　Why are they never around
　When I need a shoulder
Oh, when will I stop feeling so blue

Questionnaire mix-up

Sam has written a list of questions which form a character questionnaire. They run on, one after the other, but have got mixed up with other, incorrectly punctuated pieces. Can you pick the right line, from each batch of three, to follow from the previous one?

1　a) How old are

2　a) the boys in the team. How would you describe
　　b) you? How would you describe
　　c) your two sisters, would you describe

3　a) yourself? Are you
　　b) yourself and your sister. Are you
　　c) your best friend. Is she

4　a) generous or selfish. I wonder whether you feel
　　b) mean and difficult, We wonder if you like
　　c) lively or quiet? We wonder if you like

5　a) jeans or skirts best. Are
　　b) red or pink nail polish best? Are
　　c) country and western music? Are

6　a) your eyes blue
　　b) you short or tall.
　　c) your eyes dark or light.

7　a) green or hazel? Can you
　　b) , green or hazel? Can you
　　c) green or hazel. Can you

8　a) tell me how how often you play tennis. Do you like
　　b) ride a bike. Do you enjoy
　　c) swim, play tennis and ride a bike? You enjoy

9　a) playing the piano, don't you? Do you prefer
　　b) playing the piano, don't you... Do you prefer
　　c) playing the piano? Do you prefer

10　a) sports to quiet things like reading.
　　b) playing computer games or watching TV?
　　c) playing computer, games or watching TV?

13

I'm scared!

exclamation mark

The exclamation mark is a vertical line over a dot. It can go on the end of a sentence instead of a full stop. An exclamation mark shows that the sentence expresses a strong feeling such as anger, delight, surprise or fear.

When do you use one?

Exclamation marks are optional. You can always end the type of sentence described above with a full stop.

There is no rule about this. The best advice is to use few exclamation marks. If you use too many, they have less effect. Use one on the end of short expressions (such as *Ouch!*), and where you want to draw attention to the strength of feeling.

Look at this example: *What a storm! It was unbelievable! The thunder and lightning were continuous, the sky was black and the rain came down in torrents! Within seconds, we were soaked! I have never been so scared!*

With fewer exclamation marks, the effect is stronger: *What a storm! It was unbelievable. The thunder and lightning were continuous, the sky was black and the rain came down in torrents. Within seconds, we were soaked. I have never been so scared.*

Where you place exclamation marks changes the meaning slightly by drawing attention to the sentences that have them. In this piece of writing, you could underline the scary effect of the storm by putting one on the end: *I have never been so scared!*

Short expressions

A tip for dealing with more than one expression of surprise, anger and so on is to use a mixture of commas and exclamation marks. For example, you should avoid writing *Wow! How brilliant!* Instead, write *Wow, how brilliant!*

It can also go on the end of an order or a short expression to show that they are said loudly or with lots of feeling:

Ouch! **What a stupid thing to do!** **Call the police!**

Remember, as the exclamation mark is used instead of a full stop, it is followed by a capital letter.

One only

Where you want an exclamation mark, one is always enough. You may see two or three used, but you should only use one.

—— Overkill ——

Copy this newspaper article, cutting eight exclamation marks and replacing two of these with commas. (Adjust capital letters as necessary.)

What a calamity!!! Dire is to lose its railway station toilet unless urgent action is taken. This, at least, is what the Association of Dire Residents (ADR) fear, following their meeting with the Station's Passenger Liaison Committee (SPLC) yesterday.

According to the ADR spokesperson, Gail Bigwail, the Committee is intent on cutting costs. Losing the toilet will save exactly the amount they are looking for.

What an unnecessary, backwards step!! The shortest journey from Dire is 23 minutes, and with no toilet at Dire Central, passengers would just have to keep their legs crossed!!!

We agree with Ivor Right, also of the ADR, who points out that, with a little thought and care, small savings could be made here and there, thus allowing the toilet to be kept open. How true, Mr. Right, and how eagerly we will publicize your views! The ADR are planning a Day of Action in the near future. So cheer up, Citizens of Dire! Buy the Dire Echo every day! And we will keep you informed!!

ise! *How stunning!* What a kind man! *How unusual!*

Surprise, surprise

Dawn has come top in her class this year. Her little brother took all the messages she received and scratched out some of the punctuation. Each message should have an extra exclamation mark, comma and full stop. Copy the four messages, adding the right punctuation in each of the scratched spaces.

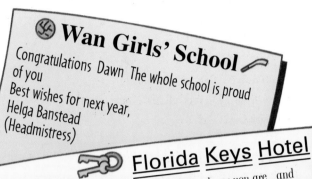

Foxes' Dale
Boarding School for Boys

Wow, you HAVE got a brain after all
I suppose I'm impressed though it's pretty horrid having to admit it
See you on Saturday, Einstein.
Charlie

Great stuff, Miss Brainypants After Lady Banstead's stunning announcement   I can only beg to remain your proud best friend
See you at volleyball, clever socks!
Di

Wan Girls' School

Congratulations Dawn The whole school is proud of you
Best wishes for next year,
Helga Banstead
(Headmistress)

Florida Keys Hotel

Dear Dawn,
You brilliant girl I just can't get over how clever you are   and I'm dying to get home from this wretched business trip so I can give you the hug you deserve
Watch your brothers. Charlie will be green with envy but OK.
Jamie will hate you getting all the attention!
See you on Saturday.
Lots of love,
Mum

Fruit machine roundup

This puzzle gives you a chance to test yourself on all the punctuation explained so far in this book (from page 3 to here).

Someone has played on the fruit machine and jumbled the last two parts of each sentence. Copy the first pieces, then work out which centre pieces and which end pieces match up with them. (Look closely at the punctuation.)

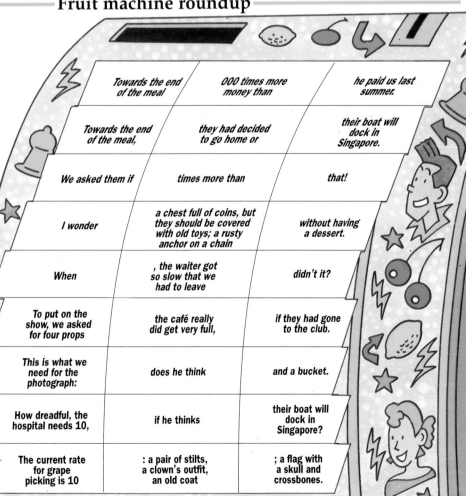

Towards the end of the meal	000 times more money than	he paid us last summer.
Towards the end of the meal,	they had decided to go home or	their boat will dock in Singapore.
We asked them if	times more than	that!
I wonder	a chest full of coins, but they should be covered with old toys; a rusty anchor on a chain	without having a dessert.
When	, the waiter got so slow that we had to leave	didn't it?
To put on the show, we asked for four props	the café really did get very full,	if they had gone to the club.
This is what we need for the photograph:	does he think	and a bucket.
How dreadful, the hospital needs 10,	if he thinks	their boat will dock in Singapore?
The current rate for grape picking is 10	: a pair of stilts, a clown's outfit, an old coat	; a flag with a skull and crossbones.

The apostrophe looks like a comma, but it goes higher on the line. The top of it lines up with the tops of letters like *l* and *k*.

apostrophe

Annie's cat is at the door.

Two uses

The apostrophe is used in two ways:
1 It can show that some letters are missing (as in *The cat's at the door*, where *cat's* stands for *cat is*). This is explained on page 18.
2 It can also show possession (who something belongs to), as in the example, *Annie's cat*.

's for possession

To show who something belongs to, you normally add *'s* to the owner's name. Here are some examples of this possessive *'s*:

Fred's shirt (the shirt that belongs to Fred, or the shirt of Fred)

the teacher's car (the car that belongs to the teacher, or the car of the teacher)

King Midas's gold (the gold belonging to King Midas, or the gold of King Midas)

the actress's wig (the wig belonging to the actress, or the wig of the actress)

This *'s* is correct for all nouns (naming words) when they are singular. Singular means there is only one, as opposed to plural (more than one). For example, *car* is singular (only one), and *cars* is plural (more than one). Look at the examples above and notice that even singular nouns which end in *s* add *'s*.

Plural nouns

Most nouns have an extra *s* on the end when they are plural (more than one). For example: *parents*. To show possession for these, you add only an apostrophe*. Here are some examples:
my parents' car (the car that belongs to my parents)
the Smiths' car (the car that belongs to the Smiths)

Unusual plurals

A few nouns do not have an extra *s* or *es* when they are plural, but change in another way. For example: *child, children*. To show possession for these, add *'s*. For example: *the children's room*.

Spotting possessives

To tell if a noun with an *s* needs an apostrophe, try using *of*. For example, for *Annie's cat*, you can say the *cat of Annie*. This means it is possessive and needs *'s*.

───── **Filling the gap** ─────

For these sentences, which word shown in blue fits the gap?

1 His ... house is in Armadillo.
parents'/parents
2 Their ... bedrooms are all in the attic.
children's/childrens'
3 We ended up in the ... worst restaurant.
towns/town's/towns'
4 My ... colours are scarlet, blue and yellow.
teams/teams'/team's
5 My favourite ... annual tour starts next week.
bands/band's/bands'
6 Mrs ... next-door neighbour is a retired filmstar.
Jones/Jones's
7 Of this ... two radios, only one is working.
ship's/ships'/ships's
8 The conductor would not let us onto the ... top deck.
buses'/bus's
9 By the end of the match, the 13 ... energy had completely run out.
player's/players'/players
10 The ... garage had been emptied overnight.
Brown's/Browns'

*For nouns which end in *ch, sh, s, x* or *z*, and a few which end in *o*, add *es*. For some of those ending in *y*, the *y* changes to *i* and you add *es*. For example: *bush, bushes; baby, babies*.

s voice   the Smiths' car   my band's manager   Fred's hat

Get the facts right

Look at the words and pictures below. For the first set, the correct phrase is *the cats' basket*. Add apostrophes to make the remaining eleven phrases. Make sure that the nouns in your phrases change to plural where necessary to match the pictures.

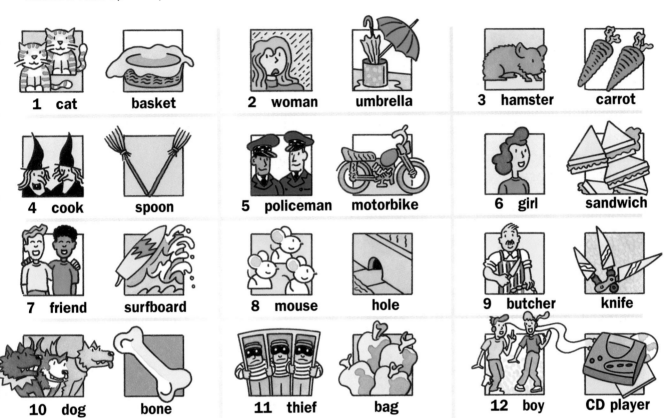

1 cat   basket

2 woman   umbrella

3 hamster   carrot

4 cook   spoon

5 policeman   motorbike

6 girl   sandwich

7 friend   surfboard

8 mouse   hole

9 butcher   knife

10 dog   bone

11 thief   bag

12 boy   CD player

Photo album

Of the two sentences given for each photo, only one matches the picture? Can you work out which?

A1 My cousins' hair is jet black.
A2 My cousin's hair is jet black.

B1 The girl's room is blue.
B2 The girls' room is blue.

C1 My uncles' vans are purple.
C2 My uncle's vans are purple.

D1 All the baby's clothes are stripy.
D2 All the babies' clothes are stripy.

E1 My aunt's eyes are green.
E2 My aunts' eyes are green.

F1 Their dogs' bowls are yellow.
F2 Their dog's bowls are yellow.

Contractions

Page 16 explains how you use apostrophes to show who something belongs to (as in *Annie's cat*). They are also used to show where there is a contraction. A contraction is when some letters are missing in a word because it is said in a shortened form. In the examples on the right, *cat's* and *can't* are contractions. They are short for *cat is* and *cannot*.

> **Her cat's at the door.**

> **I can't see it.**

Common ones

Most contractions are short forms of verbs. Here are some examples:
'm short for *am* (as in *I'm a gym teacher*);
's short for *is* (as in *He's a maths teacher*), or short for *has* (as in *She's left*).

Contractions are also often short forms of a verb used with *not*. For example, *isn't* is short for *is not* (*She isn't here*).

Avoiding them

Contractions are part of spoken English. Never use them in essays and written homework, nor in formal writing (letters asking for information or work, for example). You can use them in written English if you are writing something informal like a message or letter to a friend, or when you are writing down what someone said.

Unusual ones

A few expressions, such as *o'clock*, are contractions which are always written with an apostrophe. This is because the full expression is out of date and is no longer used. *O'clock* stands for *of the clock*.

A few family names are also written with an apostrophe. These are usually names which come originally from Ireland, for example: *O'Connor*.

Trouble shooting

People often make mistakes with apostrophes. To help you to avoid this, here is a summary of when to use them.

1 To show possession:
* for singular nouns, add *'s*.
Example: the *teacher's pet*;
* for plural nouns that end in s, add an apostrophe after the s.
Example: *the three teachers' pet* (the pet of the three teachers);
* for plural nouns that do not end in *s*, add *'s* (as for singular nouns).
    Example: *the children's room*.
* Expressions such as *baker's, doctor's* and *at Jessie's* are possessives. They are short for *baker's shop, doctor's surgery, at Jessie's house*, and so on. You must write them with *'s* on the end.

2 Use an apostrophe to show a contraction. Examples are *I'd* (for *I had, I should* or *I would)*, *won't* (for *will not)*, *can't* (for *cannot)*, *you've* (for *you have)*, *she's* (for *she has*) and *don't* (for *do not)*. Contractions are common in spoken English. Avoid them when writing, except in informal writing.

3 Do not confuse *its* and *it's*:
* *its* means "belonging to it", as in *Look at the bike! Its saddle is broken*. In this sense, *its* does not have an apostrophe;
* *it's* is the contraction of *it is*.

If you are in any doubt, try putting *it is* where you are having the problem. If the sentence makes sense, *it's* is right. If not, try *his* (or *her*). If the sentence now makes sense, then *its* is correct. For example, in *Its saddle is broken*, you cannot replace *its* by *it is*, but *His saddle is broken* makes sense, so *its* is correct.

——— Incy-wincy ———

Fill the gaps in this description with either *it, its* or *it's*.

Like all spiders, ... has eight legs. ... overall length is about that of a human hand. The web ...makes out of ... own silk is so strong that even small animals get trapped in .... not able to eat solid food, so ... fills ... prey with special juices to turn ... into liquid ... can eat.

isn't shan't don't didn't can't isn't shan't don't didn't

Chatterbox contractions

These speech bubbles each contain one or more contractions (words with letters missing). Rewrite the words in full without the contractions.

> Maria's paintbrushes aren't in the same box as yours.

> The baker's is closed and the supermarket doesn't sell Mr Duff's doughnuts.

> It's not worth mending my tennis racket: all its strings are broken and the handle's cracked.

> I won't be allowed to come unless you'll give me a lift home.

> There's nothing on that they'd really like to see.

> Its streets are so quiet and dull, especially when it's raining.

> I'd rather go to Suzie's, if she's home.

> They'd all gone by the time we got there.

> That baker's a surly man.

> They've gone to the doctor's.

Filling apostrophes

There are eleven apostrophes missing in this message. Copy it out and add them in.

> Is going to the dentists a nightmare for your child? Come to us. Were the childrens specialists. Some dentists terrify kiddies. Its their approach thats all wrong. Ours is sensitive and fun. Our surgeries look like kids playrooms, but theyre equipped with the latest technology so everythings as quick, painless and easy as possible - even fillings are fun here. Theres constant music and we tell the kids spooky or fun stories while we work. Well take good care of your childrens health and looks without giving cause for fear and tears!

Crime busters

Read Sergeant Jones's notes on the suspected burglary at the Harrises' bungalow. Decide which word or expression from the red list below fits each gap. (Use each one once only.)

Mr and Mrs 1 are away on business. The 2 daughter got home from school at six. As soon as she put her 3 in the 4 front door, she knew something was wrong. One of the 5 glass panels was cracked. A brave girl, she walked in.

Everything appeared normal except that all the inside 6 were open, whereas some are usually kept closed, and her 7 dogs weren't barking. The 8 behaviour was odd and they seemed groggy. "9 very unusual. 10 always waiting by the door because 11 want to go out." She thinks the 12 had been doped.

Other strange things were that the garage 13 usual hiding place had been searched, a camera was missing from her 14 wardrobe, and in the study, the computer was on and the message on 15 screen said: "Now 16 time to reveal the truth." The Harrises' daughter said her 17 will be back tonight.

Before leaving, I checked the other 18 and all the windows, which all looked fine. The other 19 on the street had not been disturbed.

Harrises' / door's / doors / bungalow's / parents' / dogs' / it's / It's / doors / They're / key / dogs / they / Harris / bungalows / its / parents' / key's / parents

19

When you write the words that someone said, you use quotation marks to show where their words begin and end. The opening marks look like two upside-down apostrophes. The closing ones look like two apostrophes. Quotation marks are also quite often called speech marks, inverted commas or quotes.

John said, "They've quotation found the way out." marks

All about direct speech

Direct speech is when you write spoken words in quotation marks. The words go inside the quotation marks with their punctuation, though you sometimes have to adjust the punctuation a little.

The verb that introduces the spoken words (*say*, *ask*, *whisper* and so on) can go first, last, or in the middle. Here you can see how the punctuation should be in each case:

1 If the verb is first:

> two capital letters: one at the start of the sentence, and one where the spoken words start

He said, "They've found the way out."

> comma* at the end of the introduction, before "

> full stop before "

2 If the verb is last:

> one capital letter only

"They've found the way out," he said.

> comma after the spoken words, before " (replacing the full stop that the spoken words ended with)

3 If the verb is in the middle:

> comma within the quotation marks

"From what I can see," he said, peering into the binoculars, "they've found the way out."

> comma before "

> one full stop at the end, before "

Think of the words in quotation marks and the words that introduce them as a sentence. Whichever of the three patterns you follow, the sentence starts with a capital letter and ends with a full stop (or *?* or *!*). If the closing quotation marks are on the end (as in 1 and 3), the full stop (or *?* or *!*) is within them.

Ending with ? and !

If the spoken words end with a question mark or exclamation mark, this is what you do:
He asked, "Have you found the way out?"
He said, "They've found the way out!"

> ? or ! before " (no need for a full stop)

"Have you found the way out?" he asked.
"They've found the way out!" he said.

> no capital letter after ? or ! (notice that this breaks the usual rule about having a capital letter after ! and ?)

Dialogue

When you write a dialogue (two or more people's spoken words), you can start a new paragraph (see page 24) each time you switch to a new speaker. This helps to make clear who is speaking:
"Who did you say?" she asked.
"I said Fred, but I meant Ted!" he answered, laughing.

Indirect speech

There is another way of writing people's words, called indirect, or reported, speech. This is when you report the words that someone said, rather than giving their exact spoken words. For example:
John said that they had found the way out. In indirect speech, you never use quotation marks.

*A colon is sometimes used here instead of the comma: *He said: "They've found the way out."*

"Now," he cried, "jump." He said, "Never!" "Now," he

What was that?

Write what these six people are saying, using direct speech. For each one, start with *he* or *she said* (or *he* or *she asked*, in the case of questions). Then do the same again, but put *he/she said* or *he/she asked* at the end. Try to get all the punctuation right.

> **Right, put your pens down now, please!**

> **Carol's taken my pen.**

> **Jamie was copying Tracy's answers.**

> **I can't believe how hard that was!**

> **Did you hear about Ros and Kate?**

> **I've left my lunch box at home!**

Adventure diary

In total, there are 12 sets of quotation marks missing from these diary entries. Read them through, then copy out all the sections that need quotation marks, adding these in (and adjusting the punctuation to go with them).

Great Rocks Holiday Centre

Day 1

Now I'm here. I'm sure I shall be all right. Everyone's really friendly and no one looks the real outdoors type. I'm sharing a room with a girl called Claire.

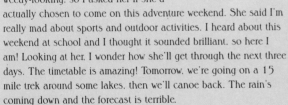

We chatted a bit before this evening's meal. She is thin, pale and weedy-looking, so I asked her if she'd actually chosen to come on this adventure weekend. She said I'm really mad about sports and outdoor activities. I heard about this weekend at school and I thought it sounded brilliant, so here I am! Looking at her, I wonder how she'll get through the next three days. The timetable is amazing! Tomorrow, we're going on a 15 mile trek around some lakes, then we'll canoe back. The rain's coming down and the forecast is terrible.

Day 2

The day was so full. Claire and I still didn't get a chance to chat much. When we were setting off this morning, Alice, our instructor, asked her why is your backpack twice the size of everyone else's? My strange room-mate answered because I want to get really fit! Alice said leave a few things behind. Claire just shook her head and laughed.

I'm too tired to stay up writing about it all. Tomorrow we're going to do some climbing and abseiling. Aaagh!

Day 3

Well, the weekend is nearly over. Tonight, we're going to have a barbecue by the lake. Today was awesome. The abseiling was just as scary as I'd thought, and when it was all over, Alice told me you'll have to come back with Claire in the summer. You make a great team! When I asked her why, she said you're over-cautious but Claire encourages you. Claire's reckless but you keep her in check.

At the barbecue, I got a chance to talk to Claire a bit more. She's amazing. I love doing all this she told me while we were stuffing our faces because I broke an arm and a leg in a skiing accident last winter and I got so fed up having to stay indoors all the time.

Home again

How was your weekend? everyone keeps asking me. I just say I was best at everything. You know me! What I don't tell them about is the nightmares I keep having.

A few hours after I'd got home, Claire phoned to ask if I want to go back to Great Rocks with her in August. Well I answered I'll think about it and phone you back soon. Whoops, I don't have her phone number!

I stepped across the fast-running stream (as the picture shows).

brackets   hyphen

There is no room left — I said: no room!

dash

Brackets

Brackets are pairs of curved lines which you use around words in order to separate them from the rest of a sentence.
For example:
My ant project is finished, but Jan's Dad (an insect specialist, as I found out) said he would look at it before I hand it in*.

Usually, the words in brackets give extra detail or an explanation.

With brackets, the punctuation depends on whether you choose to write the words in brackets as part of a sentence or as a separate sentence.

If they are part of a sentence, any punctuation that belongs to the sentence goes outside the brackets. For example:
Entries must reach us by 22 May (any received later will not be valid).

If they form a separate sentence, the punctuation goes inside the brackets:
Entries must reach us by 22 May. (Entries received later will not be valid.)

Dashes

A dash is a short horizontal line used on its own or as part of a pair**. It is best avoided, especially in formal writing.

Dashes have about the same use as brackets. In informal writing or in direct speech, you can use them instead of brackets. Use two dashes if the extra words are in the middle of the sentence, as in *They want to visit Paris — I can see why — on their way to Geneva.* Use one dash if the extra words are at the end: *They want to visit Paris — I can understand why.*

Hyphens

A hyphen is like a dash, but shorter. Its main use is to join two or more words to show they should be read as one word with its own meaning. For example: *on-the-spot fines, short-term deal.*

Words like this, made from two or more words, are called compound words. Some gradually become accepted as new words that you write without a hyphen, For example: *offside, seaweed, flashback.*

There are no firm rules to tell you when to join words up or when to link them with hyphens. You will often have to check compound words in a dictionary.

Hyphen guidelines

1 Use hyphens if the meaning is unclear or wrong without them:
A *two-month-old kittens*
B *two month-old kittens*

2 Use hyphens to join words that must be read as one and that are before a noun they describe: *a long-overdue award.*
3 Use a hyphen to join a verb ending in *ing* or *ed* with another word that changes its meaning. For example: *well-tuned, mind-boggling.* (The exception is if the other word ends in *ly*, when no hyphen is needed: *nicely worded.*)
4 Use a hyphen to join words with the same last and first letters: *grass-seed.*

In American English, more compound words are written as one word than in British English. For example: *night-time* (UK) but *nighttime* (US).

Other uses

The hyphen is used to mean *to* in expressions like *1964-1982.*

Hyphens also go on the end of a line to break up a long word for which there is not enough room. Avoid this in your writing if you can. If you do it, break the word in a place which will not make reading difficult.

It is a pa-ragraph.

It is a para-graph.

*You can often use commas instead of brackets. Use brackets when they make the writing much clearer, as in this example.
**Never use other punctuation next to a dash.

Internet link: For a link to a website where you can find out more about hyphens and dashes and try an activity, go to www.usborne-quicklinks.com

( ) - _ ( ) - _ ( ) - _ ( ) - _ ( ) - _ ( ) - _ ( ) - _ ( )

Pirates aboard game

The story below has 19 numbered gaps. Use the board on the right to complete it. For each gap, look at the strip with the matching number and select the correct piece to fill the gap. (You will probably have to look some words up in a dictionary.)

Pirate MacClaw crept up the 1 to the galleon's deck. 2 Tom Puffin, who had rowed old MacClaw across from the 3 pirate ship 4 sick with fear all the way), shivered in the boat beneath.

5 MacClaw (who had celebrated his 6 the previous night) ran across the deserted deck towards the captain's quarters. He did not blink an 7 as he caught sight of the huge cages in which the galleon's captain was reputed to keep 8 and a 9 tiger. He had other things on his mind.

Soon he was creeping into Captain Cachou's cabin 10 was fast asleep on a 11 stool opposite the door. Unfortunately, MacClaw's parrot (who had been 12 on the old pirate's left shoulder ever since he had clambered on board the galleon) suddenly screeched, "Pirate MacClaw here!" This 13 went unheard, though, for the captain was in his 14 and his head was 15.

In the 16, the pirate had the 17 leather folder firmly in his large hands and was running back down towards Tom. The boy quietly sighed with relief (and wondered how he would ever have his 18 Mission accomplished, Tom rowed them into the peaceful, safe darkness, in which the blurred outlines of the 19 soon appeared.

MacCLAW'S MISSION

1	loosely tied rope ladder	loosely-tied rope-ladder	loosely tied ropeladder
2	Mean while	Mean-while	Meanwhile,
3	nowinvisible	now invisible	now-invisible
4	(and who had felt	and who had felt	and (who had felt
5	Quietfooted	Quiet-footed	Quiet footed
6	seventieth birthday	seventieth birth day	seventieth birth-day
7	eye lid	eye-lid	eyelid
8	blood-hounds	bloodhounds	blood hounds
9	maneating	man eating	man-eating
10	— the guard	(the guard	— the guard —
11	three legged	threelegged	three-legged
12	solidly-perched	solidly perched	solidlyperched
13	ill timed squawk	illtimed squawk	ill-timed squawk
14	bathtub	bath-tub	bath tub
15	under water	under-water	underwater
16	twinkling of an eye	twinkling-of-an-eye	twinkling of an eye —
17	longdesired	long-desired	long desired
18	grand-pa's courage).	grandpa's courage.)	grandpa's courage).
19	pirate ship	pirate-ship	pirateship

Face painting

Where should you add one pair of brackets in each of these seven instructions?

1. You will need face paints, two or three brushes and at least one sponge see Getting started on p.1.

2. Use water-based paints they cost more but give better results.

3. Sponge a yellow base onto the face brownish yellow if possible.

4. Sponge a white muzzle and chin lions have a white beard.

5. Paint a black nose joined to a black upper lip; also paint black lines around the eyes. See the illustration.

6. Paint bottom lip red and add black whiskers dots and lines as shown.

7. Brush hair up and back into a mane and sponge white streaks onto it. These will easily wash out.

If the layout of your writing (the way it is placed on the page) is cramped, it is hard to read. Here are some guidelines to help you present it neatly. You can also find out how to lay out letters.

Margins

Margins are the spaces which you leave on the left and right with no writing in them.

The left-hand margin should be straight (you can draw a line in with a ruler), and it is often a little wider than the right-hand margin. You can make the right-hand margin straight too, although you may end up with awkward gaps between the words.

Each new paragraph starts at the same distance from the left-hand margin.

Someone had to go down. The divers all looked terrified. Titch volunteered.

She lowered herself into the sea and let go of the ladder. She soon located the wreck, a gloomy shape beneath her. She found the right porthole. It was shut tight.

She tugged on the frame. All of a sudden, it was pushed from inside. An unknown diver's face appeared.

Paragraphs

A paragraph is a short section of writing within a longer piece. Each new paragraph starts a little way from the left margin (called indenting).

There are no rules to say where you should start a new paragraph. Usually, you do so when you move to a new subject or a new aspect of the same subject.

Formal letters

There are two styles to choose from.

Style 1: indented paragraphs

Address of person you are writing to

your address

Fun Products,
4 Creek Road,
London, SE8 3PH
10 July 2000

date

Mr Jensen,
The Magic Shop,
36 Park Avenue,
Barmouth,
Gwynedd, GW7 2PL

comma (*Dear Sir* or *Dear Madam* if you don't know the name)*

Dear Mr Jensen,
    On 6 June, I sent you a sample of our latest false moustache.
    Please either let me know your response or return the sample to me.
    Yours sincerely,
Katie Katz
Katie Katz

Sign, and type or write your name clearly.

Style 2: everything lined up on the left, except your address**

Fun Products,
4 Creek Road,
London, SE8 3PH
10 July 2000

Mr Jensen,
The Magic Shop,
36 Park Avenue,
Barmouth,
Gwynedd, GW7 2PL

Dear Mr Jensen,
On 6 June, I sent you a sample of our latest false moustache.

Please either let me know your response or return the sample to me.
Yours sincerely,
Katie Katz
Katie Katz

Leave a little space between paragraphs.

Informal letters

For letters to friends or family, you can follow either style. You leave out the person's address, though, and you could also leave out your own. End with something like *With love from*, *See you soon* or *With best wishes*:

7 Mermaid Lane,
Rye,
East Sussex,
Tuesday 12 August

Dear Ben,
    The week in Dorset was brilliant. Many thanks once again for organizing it.
    Did you find Lucy's lead? I'm sure I left it in your car. Please bring it down on Sunday.
Love to you all,
Ray

Envelopes

There are two possible styles for the address on an envelope:

Mr Jensen,
The Magic Shop,
36 Park Avenue,
Barmouth,
Gwynedd, GW7 2PL.

Mr Jensen,
The Magic Shop,
36 Park Avenue,
Barmouth,
Gwynedd, GW7 2PL.

Addresses

On the letters and envelopes shown here, all the addresses have commas. This punctuation can be left out, even in formal letters.

*If you don't know whether you are writing to a man or woman, put *Dear Sir/Madam*. In this case, end with *Yours faithfully*.
**Notice that this breaks the usual rule about starting new paragraphs away from the left margin.

Internet link: For a link to a website where you can find out how to write a business letter, go to **www.usborne-quicklinks.com**

es *envelopes letters margins paragraphs addresses*

Letter box

Lay out these two letters properly. Do letter 1 following style 1 and letter 2 following style 2 (see opposite page).

Letter 1

Date: 7 May 2000

From: you (at your own address)

To: the manager of an ice-rink. You know the manager is a man, but you don't know his name.

The ice-rink's address: Ice World, Coldharbour Street, London N4 1RT.

What your letter says (write it in a single paragraph): I came skating yesterday and I left my shoes in the changing room. Please keep them for me if you find them. I will pick them up next week.

Letter 2

Date: 6 May 2000

From: you (at your own address)

To: Mrs Graham, the manageress of a supermarket.

The supermarket's address: Cheapstore, 106 Kiln Road, Birmingham BH7 6AJ.

What your letter says (break this into two paragraphs): Last week, I bought a jar of instant coffee from Cheapstore which I had to return. The coffee had a thick layer of green mould on the top. Please could you contact me about this matter as soon as possible? You said that I would hear from you within 48 hours, but I still have not.

Tiebreaker

To win trips to a city of their choice, the entrants in this competition had to give their reasons for wanting to go there. Here are the three winning entries.

Can you split each one into three paragraphs?

Tiebreaker Competition

The city I most want to visit is Cairo. This is because the Sphinx and the Pyramids are just on the outskirts, and I would like to see them. I did a project on ancient Egypt and I built a model of the Sphinx. My model is small and new. I would like to stand in front of the real Sphinx, which is huge and ancient. Another reason for going to Cairo is to see the Nile. This is the longest river in the world, and if I visited Cairo, I could walk across it, using a bridge of course!

My best friend has moved to London, and my biggest hobby is history. Because of this, I want to visit London. My friend lives near the British Museum. He says it is full of exciting things to see, and wants to show me some seventh century Anglo-Saxon treasure there. I only know London from books. I would especially love to visit the Tower and the Houses of Parliament.

I am fascinated by buildings and one day I want to become an architect. I live on a cattle ranch in Oregon and I have never seen any tall buildings. The city I most want to visit is New York. Here I would see some of the oldest and most famous skyscrapers in the world. I could also see the wonderful skyline that they make. I have been saving my pocket money to go to New York for three years, but I still have not got enough. I hope I win this competition, because then I can go right away and I can buy a camera with the money I have saved.

Internet link: For a link to a website where you can test whether you know where to use capital letters, go to **www.usborne-quicklinks.com**

A B C D E **Capital letters** F G H I J

capital letters (in red)

small or "lower case" letters (in blue)

Capitals checklist

Use a capital letter
• after a full stop, an exclamation mark or a question mark*;
• to write the word *I* (meaning *me*);

Also use a capital letter at the start of
• a sentence;
• months, days of the week and special days: *in January, on Monday, Easter, Thanksgiving*;
• people's names and titles: *Jill Page, Mr Fisher, Doctor Fellows, Queen Anne.* If *doctor* (or a title such as *queen, prince, duke* and so on) is used without a name, only use a capital letter if you are referring to the title of a particular person.

For example: *the Queen of England.* Use a lower case (small letter) when you are using a title in a general sense, such as: *every queen of England since 1700*;
• place names: *Sydney, California, Germany.* Words that are part of a place name start with a capital letter: *Great Salt Lake.* Words that come from place names: *a Californian, in German*;
• street names and names of buildings: *Park Lane, Ferry Street, the Eiffel Tower*;
• brand names and names of companies and organizations: *a Ford, Bird's Eye, the Foreign Office*;
• titles of books, films, songs and so on. You often also use a capital letter at the beginning of each important word in these titles: *The War of the Planets.*

Unwanted capitals

Do not use a capital letter
• at the start of the points of the compass (*Head north!*), unless they are part of a place name (*the North Pole*) or refer to a place (*the East*);
• for the seasons: *summer.*

Capital spy

Bill Spanner is jotting down a conversation that he is listening in to. Can you add the 36 capital letters that are needed?

i've arranged a meeting with two members of the dark shadow gang. it will be in a bar called the stag. it's on wincott street, just west of the junction with gilbert road, close to waterloo station. they've promised to turn up on monday at seven, on condition that i bring only you, prince baklava. we must not let anyone else know about this meeting, prince, and i mean that! don't tell princess baklava about it. they're a dangerous mob. they want us both there because they're hungarian and their english is not perfect. i can translate for you if necessary. be on time, won't you? we can meet in the street outside the stag. park your jaguar nearby and i'll look out for it. i'll wear my winter coat with the secret pockets, in case anything goes wrong.

Extras

Here are a few other signs and marks which you will see used.

[ ] Square brackets: these usually go around a comment that has been added to a piece of writing, as in *They* [the people she met in Mexico] *are coming over.*

& This sign is called an **ampersand**. It stands for and.

{ Brace: this can also be used the other way round:**}**. It is used in tables or notes to show the various parts of something. For example:

Subjects { Art French Physics

*If the full stop is used to show an abbreviation, there is no capital letter after it: *See you Tues. morning.* Exclamation marks and question marks can be followed by a small letter in direct speech (see page 20).

Page 3

Testing correspondence
There are nine full stops, nine commas, one colon, one semicolon, one exclamation mark, one question mark, four quotation marks, three hyphens and one apostrophe.

Pages 4-5

Pen problems
I'll be home late from school today, **Mum**. After volleyball practice, Miss Mussly wants to discuss plans for our sports **day**. See you at about 6 **p.m.** (Please feed Misty as soon as you get **in**. Because of the kittens, I don't think she should have to wait until **6**.)

Costly dots
SORRY I LET YOU DOWN IN **INVERNESS**. I'LL EXPLAIN WHEN I SEE **YOU**. MY MONEY BELT WAS STILL IN YOUR BACKPACK WHEN YOU LEFT IN A **HUFF**. PLEASE MEET ME FORT WILLIAM STATION ON SAT 8PM RIGHT OF LEFT-LUGGAGE LOCKERS.

Drifter's diary
Up at 11 a.m. I didn't **wash**. My sisters had left the bathroom in such a state that I didn't feel like **it**. I went over to Jo Drone's Café for a hotdog because Dad was retiling the kitchen **floor**. I just love that hot yellow **mustard**. Teeny Tina came by for me later and we spent the whole afternoon at the **D.J. Club**. On my way home I bumped into my old classmate Sally Straite in Suburb **Lane**. **When** I told her about how bored I felt, she told me to pull myself together and perhaps get a summer **job**. **She** suggested I start by keeping a diary. Sally thinks that problems I have to iron out will soon become **clear**. All I have to do is keep a diary for a few days and then read it **through**. **She** reckons the problems will soon leap off the page at **me**. Sally's tel. number is 666 3333. **She** said I can ring her whenever I need some moral **support**. I'm going to clean up the bathroom **now**. Then I'm going to have a bath and go to **bed**. It's 10 p.m.

Pointless
The five sentences which should end with a full stop are 2, 3, 4, 9 and 10.

Dotty dramas
I read the article in yesterday's Echo about the great pearl **robbery**. I was on that train and am writing to let you know what I **know**. **There** were hardly any passengers on the **train**. **In** my carriage, there was only one **man**. I noticed him because he had six briefcases and looked very **nervous**. I soon dozed **off**. **All** of a sudden, I woke up to the sound of terrible **shouts**. **A** woman with a black mask over her face rushed towards me and threw a pile of prawn and mayonnaise sandwiches in my face and all over my **clothes**. **Then** she climbed out of the window onto the **platform**. **The** woman disappeared into the night while I started trying to wipe off the prawns and mayonnaise. **At** this point, I discovered there were lots of blue pearls mixed in with the **food**. I scraped as much as I could into a plastic bag and got off the **train**. **Nobody** noticed me go in all the **commotion**. **Now** that I have read about what happened to the man with the briefcases, I want to hand in the **pearls**. **You** can phone me on 867 2382.

Pages 6-7

Two by two

A   The apples, which were red, had worms in them.
B   The apples which were red had worms in them.
C   The boys who were wearing red all had black hair.
D   The boys, who were wearing red, all had black hair.
E   The ham, which was cold, came with salad.
F   The ham which was cold came with salad.

A comma or two
1   My brother is **lazy**, rude and arrogant.
2   Many people will read this **story**, although it is very badly written.
3   Stefie has brought **flowers**, ice cream and chocolates.
4   **Meanwhile**, Susie was cycling home.
5   I took the books which were **old**, torn and **shabby**, but left the good ones for my mother.
6   The three bands that were playing were Sound and **Emotion**, Billy and the **Cheesemakers**, and the Blue Moon Band.
7   He waved at **Lisa**, who was watching from the **window**, and walked down the street.
8   The rugby **players**, who were **exhausted**, limped off the pitch together.

Lily's list
Chemist's: new **toothbrush**, aspirin and soap.
Butcher's: **sausages**, bacon and a leg of lamb.
Supermarket: **milk**, **butter**, **eggs**, **flour**, **sugar**, **pasta**, tins of sardines, and ice cream.
Greengrocer's: **apples**, **pears**, **bananas**, **beans**, carrots and broccoli.
Baker's: five bread rolls and two loaves of bread.
Hardware shop: six **short**, sturdy nails and a small hammer.

Comma commotion
These Cosifit ear muffs are warm, **comfortable and** suitable for anyone from 6 to 60! The adjustable head strap means that **however big** or small your head may be, Cosifit ear **muffs will** always fit!

This latest addition to the **Supertec computer game** series is the most exciting, challenging and **absorbing yet!** Can you help Hoghero in his desperate **battle for** control of the universe? Help him stop **Miteymouse from** conquering the world!

Every **trendy teenager** needs a Staralarm! When you go to bed, just set the alarm by choosing a time and a voice - the voice of your **favourite pop** star. What better way to wake up than to the sound of Kool Malone, **Freddy** and the Freezers or Ritchy Roon?

Pages 8-9

Mix and match

Andy and his parents have moved to Gap,/ which is in France.

Jan and her family have moved to Arcola/, which is in Canada.

I thought it over/ and quickly decided on a course of action.

He gave me some sound advice,/ but I still could not make up my mind.

In the late afternoon,/ I decided to go to the police station.

After the detective's visit/, I no longer felt in the mood to work.

The man wrinkled up his nose in disdain/, then grudgingly guided them down the dark alley.

The woman looked down her nose at them,/ but agreed to show them the documents.

Stop gap

1 Live coverage of this fascinating sporting event will begin on Radio Livewire **at 6**.
2 There were **18,000** people at the **concert**, so our chances of bumping into **Gemma**, Jim and Sam were very **slight**.
3 **Disheartened**, the explorers began their return **journey**, setting **off...**
4 In early Roman **times**, theatres were built of **wood**.
5 At **last, wet**, gasping and **exhausted**, they reached the bus **shelter**.
6 The **sun**, which we had not seen for two **months**, blinded **us**.

Printer problems

Nearly all wild cats live in **rainforests**. They hunt and eat **meat**. They have very good **eyesight**, and often...

(**Cathy,** please research all the general points for the above opening **paragraph**. When you have done **so, write** them up on my **computer**. The file name is **WCL**.)

The tiger is the largest **cat**. It is extremely **strong**. It hunts for its **food**, catching large animals if it **can**. Rather than go **hungry, though,** it eats small creatures such as **frogs, ants, worms,** beetles and so on.

(**Cathy,** please also research and write the section on **leopards**. I have gathered the relevant **books, folders, cuttings,** etc. You will find them all on my **desk,** to the left of the pile of parrot **leaflets**.)

Hasty homework

For my summer holiday, I went to Agadir, a beach paradise in Morocco. I stayed in a luxury hotel with three enormous swimming pools, a cinema, two discos, a jogging track and a computer games room.

The hotel is by a beautiful, long, white beach (OR beautiful long white beach) and the bedrooms which have balconies overlook the sea. My Mum and Dad had a hard time getting to sleep because of the waves

crashing down below. My room, which had no balcony and was just around the corner, was quiet.

I did not like the pools as much as the sea, although they did have lots of truly awesome water rapids, waves and whirlpools. The two swimming pools which have lots of sun-loungers around them are always crowded. Because the third one has lanes in it for serious swimming, it is usually empty. On the beach, there were huge waves, which I loved. One morning after a storm, I saw some jellyfish on the beach.

The food was brilliant. The hotel has chefs from all over the world, so we mostly ate Chinese food and Moroccan food, which were our favourites.

Even though we only spent a day there, our visit to Marrakesh was the highlight of the whole holiday. It is a really exciting town, and the markets and tiny ancient streets (OR tiny, ancient streets) are full of weird things like carpets, olives and spices all piled up, leather bags and sandals.

Because it was spring and the weather was not too hot, I really enjoyed this holiday.

Pages 10-11

Fishy prizes

For the pastry, you will **need:** flour, butter [...]

For the filling, have ready the **following:** fresh prawns, shelled; crab **meat,** either fresh or from a **tin;** cream, eggs and seasoning. [...]

[...] The ingredients for the cheese sauce **are:** equal amounts of milk, cream and yogurt; a tablespoon of flour; finely grated cheddar cheese; two beaten egg yolks. Stir these [...] Don't include the **cheese:** this must go in after the sauce has thickened and is off the heat.

To assemble the **pie,** do the following: put half the potato in the bottom of an ovenproof dish; place the fish mixture on top, making sure it is well spread over all the potato; cover with the remaining **potato;** finally, pour the cheese sauce [...]

For the fishcakes, mash together these **ingredients:** poached cod, boiled potatoes and two raw eggs. Add [...] Include parsley and chives, and one of the **following:** dill, fennel, sorrel. Also add a knob of butter. Shape this mixture into [...]

For the **sauce,** mince some peeled shrimps and mix with lots of sour cream.

[...] As a main course, serve with boiled new potatoes and **broccoli;** as a starter, serve with crusty bread.

Getting it right

Washomatic for sale. This machine is a genuine bargain: it is only 12 years old; there is not a single visible patch of rust on it; last but not least, it does not leak. Phone Johnny on 324 5543.

Attention, old pen collectors: Green Silhouette pen for sale, 1952 model. Features included: original case, gold nib, embossed logo. Phone Pipa Pentop, 324 5682.

For sale or hire: garage in Bach Alley. Contact Mrs Lucas, 3 Bach Square.

Wanted: young person to deliver newspapers in Combe Park area. Must have own bike. Apply to Nat's News.

Gardener sought. The following qualifications are required: familiarity with Supermow, sound knowledge of organic vegetable growing and garden pest control. Phone 324 3344.

Hair excesses

Come to **us** for a wide range of hair care: perms, hair straightening, colour change, highlights, beading, hair extensions.
Our perms are perfect in every way: gentle, **lasting** and adapted to suit your face shape.
Choose between three wonderful shampoos: frosted yogurt and banana for dry hair; lemon and lime cocktail for greasy hair; finally, for problem hair, mango and chilli revitalizing **magic** or Brazil nut balsam.
Always follow up a shampoo with a good conditioner: this guarantees good hair condition.
Amongst our dozens of choices, we recommend **either** deep action strawberry, marigold petal extract or luxury oatmilk.
Treat yourself **to** a head massage, the ideal treatment for tired heads. You get a 15 minute massage given by an expert; generous amounts of the best head massage oils; a shampoo and blow dry.
We give you the hair shape you want. Once you have it, you will want to keep it; to help you, we stock 30 varieties of hair spray. Also in stock: hundreds of lacquers, hair **gels** and waxes.

Pages 12-13

Ask a straight question

Only number 1 is an indirect question: *I asked her if she could bring him to my party.* All the others need a question mark on the end.

Awkward questions

1   Do you live here?
2   Where were you at eleven o'clock last night?
3   What are the names of the four friends who were watching TV with you?
4   Did you or one of your friends hear anything unusual?
5   Do you have a friend called Jack?
6   Was he here last night?
7   Have you heard of the Burly Gang, a gang of thugs who hang around the neighbourhood?
8   Hasn't Jack ever mentioned them to you or boasted about being their leader?
9   Why did you lie when I asked you if you had heard anything unusual?
10 Was it you who gave Jack the key to your parents' garage so he could hide there last night?

Searching questions

One day, you'll leave, won't you?
When I asked you last summer,
You said you'd be true,
But now, I just wonder.

Why is it always me
That gets left behind?
In this state, I can't see
How life can ever be kind.

Friends are no better.
Why are they never around
When I need a shoulder?
Oh, when will I stop feeling so blue?

Questionnaire mix-up

2b), 3a), 4c), 5a), 6a), 7b), 8c), 9a), 10b).

Pages 14-15

Overkill

What a **calamity!** Dire is to lose its railway station toilet unless urgent action is taken. This, at least, is what the Association of Dire Residents (ADR) fear, following their meeting with the Station's Passenger Liaison Committee (SPLC) yesterday.
According to the ADR spokesperson, Gail Bigwail, the Committee is intent on cutting costs. Losing the toilet will save exactly the amount they are looking for.
What an unnecessary, backwards **step!** The shortest journey from Dire is 23 minutes, and with no toilet at Dire Central, passengers would just have to keep their legs **crossed!**
We agree with Ivor Right, also of the ADR, who points out that, with a little thought and care, small savings could be made here and there, thus allowing the toilet to be kept open. How true, Mr. Right, and how eagerly we will publicize your views! The ADR are planning a Day of Action in the near future. So cheer up, Citizens of **Dire, buy** the Dire Echo every **day, and** we will keep you **informed!**

Surprise, surprise

1   *Wow, you HAVE got a brain after all! I suppose I'm impressed, though it's pretty horrid having to admit it. See you on Saturday, Einstein. Charlie*
2   *Great stuff, Miss Brainypants! After Lady Banstead's stunning announcement, I can only beg to remain your proud best friend. See you at volleyball, clever socks! Di*
3   *Congratulations, Dawn! The whole school is proud of you. Best wishes for next year, Helga Banstead*
4   *Dear Dawn, You brilliant girl! I just can't get over how clever you are, and I'm dying to get home from this wretched business trip so I can give you the hug you deserve. Watch your brothers. Charlie will be green with envy but OK. Jamie will hate you getting all the attention! See you on Saturday. Lots of love, Mum*

Fruit machine roundup

1   Towards the end of the meal/, the waiter got so slow that we had to leave/ without having a dessert.
2   Towards the end of the meal,/the café really did get very full,/ didn't it?
3   We asked them if/ they had decided to go home

29

or/ if they had gone to the club.

4 I wonder/ if he thinks/ their boat will dock in Singapore.

5 When/ does he think/ their boat will dock in Singapore?

6 To put on the show, we asked for four props/ : a pair of stilts, a clown's outfit, an old coat/ and a bucket.

7 This is what we need for the photograph:/ a chest full of coins, but they should be covered with old toys; a rusty anchor on a chain/ ; a flag with a skull and crossbones.

8 How dreadful, the hospital needs 10,/ 000 times more money than/ that!

9 The current rate for grape picking is 10/ times more than/ he paid us last summer.

Pages 16-17

Filling the gap
1 His **parents'** house is in Armadillo.
2 Their **children's** bedrooms are all in the attic.
3 We ended up in the **town's** worst restaurant.
4 My **team's** colours are scarlet, blue and yellow.
5 My favourite **band's** annual tour starts next week.
6 Mrs. **Jones's** next-door neighbour is a retired filmstar.
7 Of this **ship's** two radios, only one is working.
8 The conductor would not let us onto the **bus's** top deck.
9 By the end of the match, the 13 **players'** energy had completely run out.
10 The **Browns'** garage had been emptied overnight.

Get the facts right
2 the woman's umbrellas
3 the hamster's carrots
4 the cooks' spoons
5 the policemen's motorbike
6 the girl's sandwiches
7 the friends' surfboard
8 the mice's hole
9 the butcher's knives
10 the dogs' bone
11 the thieves' bags
12 the boys' CD player

Photo album
The sentences which match the pictures are: A1, B1, C2, D2, E1 and F2.

Pages 18-19

Incy-wincy
Like all spiders, **it** has eight legs. **Its** overall length is about that of a human hand. The web **it** makes out of **its** own silk is so strong that even small animals get trapped in **it**. **It's** not able to eat solid food, so **it** fills **its** prey with special juices to turn **it** into liquid **it** can eat.

Chatterbox contractions
Maria's paintbrushes **are not** in the same box as yours.
The baker's is closed and the supermarket **does not** sell Mr. Duff's doughnuts.
It is not worth mending my tennis racket: all its strings are broken and the **handle is** cracked.
I **will not** be allowed to come unless **you will** give me a lift home.
There is nothing on that **they would** really like to see.
Its streets are so quiet and dull, especially when **it is** raining.
I would rather go to Suzie's, if **she is** home.
They had all gone by the time we got there.
That **baker is** a surly man.
They have gone to the doctor's.

Filling apostrophes
Is going to the **dentist's** a nightmare for your child? Come to us. **We're** the **children's** specialists. Some dentists terrify kiddies. **It's** their approach **that's** all wrong. Ours is sensitive and fun. Our offices look like **kids'** playrooms, but **they're** equipped with the latest technology so **everything's** as quick, painless and easy as possible - even fillings are fun here. **There's** constant music and we tell the kids spooky or fun stories while we work. **We'll** take good care of your **children's** health and looks without causing fear and tears!

Crime busters

1	**Harris**	7	**parents'**	13	**key's**
2	**Harrises'**	8	**dogs'**	14	**parents'**
3	**key**	9	**It's**	15	**its**
4	**bungalow's**	10	**They're**	16	**it's**
5	**door's**	11	**they**	17	**parents**
6	**doors**	12	**dogs**	18	**doors**
				19	**bungalows**

Page 21

What was that?
She said, "Right, put your pens down now, please!"
He said, "Carol's taken my pen."
She said, "I've left my lunch box at home!"
He said, "Jamie was copying Tracy's answers."
She said, "I can't believe how hard that was!"
She asked, "Did you hear about Ros and Kate?"
"Right, put your pens down now, please!" she said.
"Carol's taken my pen," he said.
"I've left my lunch box at home!" she said.
"Jamie was copying Tracy's answers," he said.
"I can't believe how hard that was!" she said.
"Did you hear about Ros and Kate?" she asked.

Adventure diary
This is where the quotation marks should go:
Day 1 [...] *She* **said**, *"I'm really mad about sports and outdoor activities. I heard about this weekend at school and I thought it sounded great, so here I* **am!***" Looking at her* [...]

Day 2 [...] *Alice, our instructor, asked* **her,** *"Why is your backpack twice the size of everyone* **else's?"**

My strange room-mate **answered,** *"Because I want to get really* **fit!"**

Alice **said,** *"Leave a few things* **behind."** *Claire just* [...]

Day 3 [...] *Alice told* **me,** *"You'll have to come back with Claire in the summer. You make a great* **team!"**

When I asked her why, she **said,** *"You're over cautious but Claire encourages you. Claire's reckless but you keep her in* **check."**

[...] *She's amazing. "I love doing all* **this,"** *she told me while we were stuffing our* **faces,** *"because I broke an arm and a leg in a skiing accident last winter and I got so fed up having to stay indoors all the* **time."**

[...] *"How was your* **weekend?"** *everyone keeps asking me. I just* **say,** *"I was best at everything. You know* **me!"** *What I don't tell them about* [...]

[...] *with her in August.* **"Well,"** *I answered, " I'll think about it and phone you back* **soon."**

Whoops, I don't have her phone number!

Pages 22-23

Pirates aboard game
1 loosely tied rope ladder
2 Meanwhile,
3 now invisible
4 (and who had felt
5 Quiet-footed
6 seventieth birthday
7 eyelid
8 bloodhounds
9 man-eating
10 — the guard
11 three-legged
12 solidly perched
13 ill-timed squawk
14 bathtub
15 underwater
16 twinkling of an eye
17 long-desired
18 grandpa's courage).
19 pirate ship

Face painting
1 You will need face paints, two or three brushes and at least one sponge **(see** Getting started on **p.1).**
2 Use water-based paints **(they** cost more but give better **results).**
3 Sponge a yellow base onto the face **(brownish** yellow if **possible).**
4 Sponge a white muzzle and chin **(lions** have a white **beard).**
5 Paint a black nose joined to a black upper lip; also paint black lines around the eyes. **(See** the **illustration.)**
6 Paint bottom lip red and add black whisker **(dots** and lines as **shown).**
7 Brush hair up and back into a mane and sponge white streaks onto it. **(These** will easily wash **out.)**

Pages 24-25

Letter box

your address
7 May 2000

Ice World
Cold Harbour Street
London N4 1RT

Dear Sir,
I came skating yesterday and I left my shoes in the changing room. Please keep them for me if you find them. I will pick them up next week.
Yours faithfully,
your signature
your name, clearly written

your address
6 May 2000

Mrs. Graham
Cheapstore
106 Kiln Road
Birmingham BH7 6AJ

Dear Mrs. Graham,
Last week, I bought a jar of instant coffee from Cheapstore which I had to return. The coffee had a thick layer of green mould on the top.

Please could you contact me about this matter as soon as possible? You said that I would hear from you within 48 hours, but I still have not.
Yours sincerely,
your signature
your name, clearly written

Tiebreaker
The city I most want to visit is Cairo. This is because the Sphinx and the Pyramids are just on the outskirts, and I would like to see them.

I did a project on ancient Egypt and I built a model of the Sphinx. My model is small and new. I would like to stand in front of the real Sphinx, which is huge and ancient.

Another reason for going to Cairo is to see the Nile. This is the longest river in the world, and if I visited Cairo, I could walk across it, using a bridge of course!

I am fascinated by buildings and one day I want to become an architect. I live on a cattle ranch in Oregon and I have never seen any tall buildings.

The city I most want to visit is New York. Here I would see some of the oldest and most famous skyscrapers in the world. I could also see the wonderful skyline that they make.

I have been saving my pocket money to go to New York for three years, but I still have not got enough. I hope I win this competition, because then I can go right away and I can buy a camera with the money I have saved.

My best friend has moved to London, and my biggest hobby is history. Because of this, I want to visit London.

My friend lives near the British Museum. He says it is full of exciting things to see and wants to show me some seventh century Anglo-Saxon treasure there.

I only know London from books. I would especially love to visit the Tower and the Houses of Parliament.

Page 26

Capital spy
I've arranged a meeting with two members of the **Dark Shadow Gang.** *It will be in a bar called the* **Stag.** *It's on* **Wincott Street,** *just west of the junction with* **Gilbert Road,** *close to* **Waterloo Station.** *They've promised to come on* **Monday** *at seven, on condition that* **I** *bring only you,* **Prince Baklava.** *We must not let anyone else know about this meeting,* **Prince,** *and I mean that!* **Don't** *tell* **Princess Baklava** *about it. They're a dangerous mob.* **They** *want us both there because they're* **Hungarian** *and their* **English** *is not perfect. I can translate for you if necessary.* **Be** *on time, won't you?* **We** *can meet in the street outside the* **Stag. Park** *your* **Jaguar** *nearby and I'll look for it. I'll wear my winter coat with the secret pockets, in case anything goes wrong.*

Acknowledgements

Editor: Nicole Irving
Series editor: Jane Chisholm
Series designer: Diane Thistlethwaite
Cover designer: Nicola Butler
Editorial assistance: Fiona Patchett

This edition first published in 2004 by Usborne Publishing Ltd, 83-85 Saffron Hill, London EC1N 8RT, England.
www.usborne.com